YOUR LAND
AND
MY LAND
ASIA

We Visit

SINGAPORE

John

Bankston

Mitchell Lane
PUBLISHERS
P.O. Box 196
Hockessin, Delaware 19707

YOUR LAND
AND
MY LAND
ASIA

YOUR LAND
AND
MY LAND
ASIA

We Visit

SINGAPORE

Mitchell Lane

PUBLISHERS

Printing   1   2   3   4   5   6   7   8   9

Library of Congress Cataloging-in-Publication Data
Bankston, John, 1974-
  We visit Singapore / by John Bankston.
      pages cm. — (Your land and my land: Asia)
  Includes bibliographical references and index.
  ISBN 978-1-61228-484-2 (library bound)
  1. Singapore—Juvenile literature. I. Title.
  DS609.B37 2013
  959.57—dc23
                                              2013033975
eBook ISBN: 9781612285399

PBP

Contents

Introduction

Southeast Asia is dominated by an archipelago—a stretch of water containing many islands. Lying between the Asian mainland and Australia in the Indian and Pacific Oceans, the East Indian Archipelago stretches more than 4,000 miles (6,440 kilometers) from east to west and 1,300 miles (2,100 kilometers) from north to south. Also known as the Malay Archipelago, it is the largest archipelago in the world and encompasses some 25,000 islands.

One of those islands is fairly small. It is about as long as the distance of a marathon race, or 26 miles (42 kilometers). Its total area is about four times the size of our nation's capital. It has few natural resources. Yet it is one of the wealthiest places on earth, with an urban landscape dominated by skyscrapers and high-rises.

This is Singapore. Just 85 miles north of the Equator, it consists of one main island surrounded by about 60 smaller islands.

Once run by a distant colonial power, Singapore gained its independence in 1957. The country endured the same chaos that followed independence in many other countries. Yet in a relatively short time, the country stabilized and embarked on a path to modernism which continues today.

The tallest observation wheel in the world, the Singapore Flyer looms over the Marina Sands Skypark. Each capsule holds 28 people and a complete rotation takes half an hour.

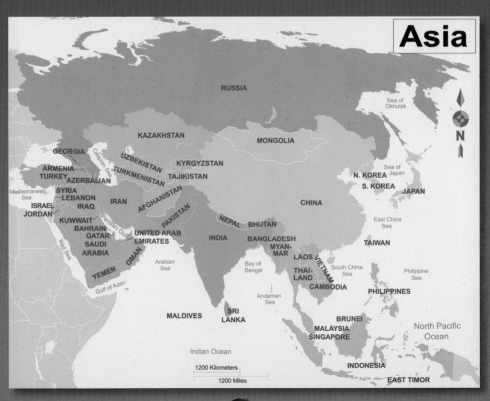

Singapore is a country of industry and skyscrapers, but it also boasts many acres of pristine land like the Singapore Botanic Gardens.

Singapore Overview

Welcome to Singapore. It may be surprising to learn that one out of three people living in Singapore is originally from somewhere else. Few other countries on Earth have been as welcoming to immigrants as Singapore. First settled by the Malays, who landed from nearby Malaya, Singapore has also been home to Chinese and Indians for centuries. Today it welcomes people from all over the world, many of whom work in local branch offices for large corporations that are based elsewhere, primarily in Europe and the United States.

People arriving here from other countries are granted permanent residency so long as they have a job. Although they cannot vote in general elections, permanent residency allows them to receive many of the same benefits—such as low-cost government housing—that are enjoyed by Singapore's citizens. Over the past decade, the numbers of native-born Singaporeans have grown by around one percent a year. Its population of permanent residents has risen by 10 percent during the same period.

FYI FACT:

The unofficial language of Singapore is "Singlish." It combines English with Chinese grammar, Malay phrases, Hokkien slang, and elements from other languages.

Singapore is world-famous for its shopping. Visitors enjoy opportunities to buy everything from locally made crafts to luxury goods and consumer products like those here in the Bugis Junction Shopping Mall.

In Singapore, people are free to worship as they wish. Singaporeans might be Buddhist, Taoist, Muslim, or Christian. They attend services in mosques, temples, or other houses of worship. Yet while religious differences have led to conflicts elsewhere in the world, in Singapore different religions have succeeded in coexisting peacefully.

It is important for people from different backgrounds to get along in Singapore. That's because the country is one of the most crowded on earth, with an average of nearly 19,000 people per square mile (7,300 per square km). Only Monaco—which is much smaller than Singapore and which has fewer than 40,000 people—has a higher population density.

People in Singapore often follow their own traditions. As a result, a "typical" Singaporean meal might consist of curry from India, dim sum from China, or even fast food from the United States. Muslim women might wear traditional head coverings, or they might dress in modern clothing. Some Chinese people use chopsticks, others don't.

Some Singaporeans worry that the lack of a single dominant culture has left the country's young people without an identity—they don't know who they are. In a place where many people routinely work six days a week and shopping is almost a competitive sport, some critics say that money is the state religion.

A desire for wealth led the country's British colonial rulers to alter the natural landscape. Jungles were torn up to create farmland, and farmland was paved over to create the city center. Because of this loss of habitat, the tigers that once roamed the island have disappeared. As author Gretchen Liu notes, "Organized tiger hunting became a lucrative sport. Apart from a $100 reward from the government for each tiger head, the flesh could be sold at a tidy sum to Chinese medicine dealers and the skin to a collector."[1] Numerous other species were also eradicated.

Despite the damage to the environment, modern Singapore has made an effort to preserve some of its remaining natural areas. It is trying to avoid what has happened in China, where increasing industrialization and a lack of green spaces have led to dangerous pollution in larger cities.

The Sungei Buloh Wetland Reserve
has benefited from Singapore's drive to
preserve wilderness areas despite the country's
growing industrialization. The Reserve welcomes
numerous species of migratory birds, including some
which fly in from as far away as Siberia.

Beautiful public gardens have showcased the island's natural beauty ever since the Singapore Botanic Gardens was founded in 1859. The extensive grounds feature sculptures by international artists alongside a marsh garden laden with water lilies, papyrus plants, and a sundial garden. In Jurong Lake, the Chinese and Japanese gardens each occupy their own island. They provide a means of escaping the urban noise and hustle, while offering an opportunity to remember that Singapore was not always filled with people. In 2013, officials applied for UNESCO World Heritage Site status. "The Singapore Botanic Gardens fulfills the criteria for World Heritage Site assessment, and is a well-loved outdoor area for Singaporeans from all walks of life," said director Nigel Taylor. "It is also significant for its interesting history that parallels Singapore's development."[2]

For a step back in time, the Bukit Timah Nature Reserve is the only place with vegetation unchanged since the British arrival nearly two centuries ago. Comprising some 400 acres (143 hectares) on the western edge of Singapore, this rain forest may be over one million years old. Several paths guide visitors through the dense brush that is filled with mammals, reptiles, bugs, and birds.

Along the northern edge of Singapore, the Sungei Buloh Wetland Preserve contains 321 acres (130 hectares) of wetland habitat and mangrove forests with 75 percent of Singapore's wildlife species represented. It is best-known for serving as a home to more than 140 different types of birds. These include the common redshank and the Pacific golden plover, which migrates all the way from Siberia to Singapore.

Located off Singapore's southern coast, Sentosa Island was originally known as Pulau Belakang Mati, which means "Island of Death from Behind." While the origins of the name aren't clear, it lived up to its name in World War II when it was a prisoner-of-war camp. The name was changed in 1972, and means "peace and tranquility." Today up to five million visitors every year enjoy its golf courses, sandy beaches, Universal Studios Singapore, and Underwater World, with more than 2,500 Asian-Pacific marine animals like pink dolphins and sharks.

SINGAPORE FACTS AT A GLANCE

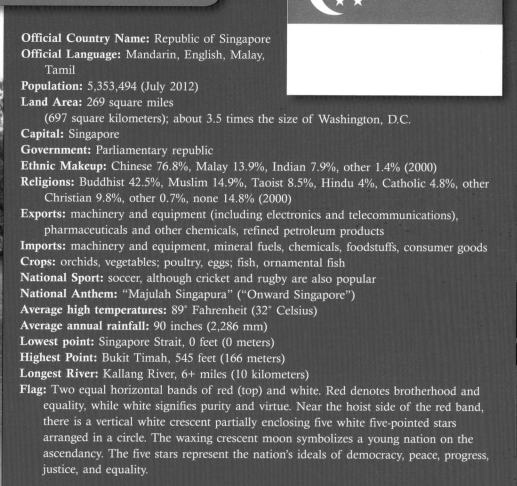

Official Country Name: Republic of Singapore

Official Language: Mandarin, English, Malay, Tamil

Population: 5,353,494 (July 2012)

Land Area: 269 square miles (697 square kilometers); about 3.5 times the size of Washington, D.C.

Capital: Singapore

Government: Parliamentary republic

Ethnic Makeup: Chinese 76.8%, Malay 13.9%, Indian 7.9%, other 1.4% (2000)

Religions: Buddhist 42.5%, Muslim 14.9%, Taoist 8.5%, Hindu 4%, Catholic 4.8%, other Christian 9.8%, other 0.7%, none 14.8% (2000)

Exports: machinery and equipment (including electronics and telecommunications), pharmaceuticals and other chemicals, refined petroleum products

Imports: machinery and equipment, mineral fuels, chemicals, foodstuffs, consumer goods

Crops: orchids, vegetables; poultry, eggs; fish, ornamental fish

National Sport: soccer, although cricket and rugby are also popular

National Anthem: "Majulah Singapura" ("Onward Singapore")

Average high temperatures: 89° Fahrenheit (32° Celsius)

Average annual rainfall: 90 inches (2,286 mm)

Lowest point: Singapore Strait, 0 feet (0 meters)

Highest Point: Bukit Timah, 545 feet (166 meters)

Longest River: Kallang River, 6+ miles (10 kilometers)

Flag: Two equal horizontal bands of red (top) and white. Red denotes brotherhood and equality, while white signifies purity and virtue. Near the hoist side of the red band, there is a vertical white crescent partially enclosing five white five-pointed stars arranged in a circle. The waxing crescent moon symbolizes a young nation on the ascendancy. The five stars represent the nation's ideals of democracy, peace, progress, justice, and equality.

Source: CIA World Factbook: Singapore
https://www.cia.gov/library/publications/the-world-factbook/geos/sn.html

A reliable source of transportation for centuries, the Chinese junk, such as this one in Singapore harbor in the 1800s, increased trade between the tiny island nation and the rest of Asia.

Early Visitors

There is little evidence of people living on the island before about 100 CE. One of the first written records dates many centuries later, in 1349, when Chinese trader Wang Dayuan described the island. By then, it had become known as Temasek, or "place surrounded by water." According to Wang, there were two primary settlements, with a total of perhaps 1,000 people. One settlement was Long-ya-men, the lair of pirates who preyed on shipping in the area. The other settlement was Banzu, a peaceful port city devoted to trade. Its inhabitants hailed originally from neighboring Malaya and distant China. Settling along terraced hillsides, they were protected behind a wall.

From the South China Sea, merchant ships passed the island before navigating the Strait of Malacca. From there, the ships entered the Indian Ocean or traveled to Middle Eastern ports. Outsiders wanted to gain control of the island and its ports because of its location.

The island eventually fell to Parameswara, a prince who lived in the Sumatran town of Pelembang. Around 1390, he left his home and attacked Singapore. According to island legend, Parameswara gave

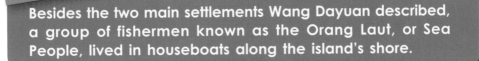

FYI FACT:

Besides the two main settlements Wang Dayuan described, a group of fishermen known as the Orang Laut, or Sea People, lived in houseboats along the island's shore.

FYI FACT:

The first "Lion City" was established in what is now Vietnam in 400 CE and served as the country's capital. The name may have been associated with Buddha, who is often shown as a lion in ancient Indian art. Some of his followers said his voice sounded like a lion's roar.

Singapore its name. He was inspired by seeing what he thought was a lion (since most lions are native to Africa, not Asia, it's likely that he actually saw a tiger). He believed that lions were a sign of good luck. He changed the name of the island from Temasek to "Singapura," which meant "Lion City."

Soon after Temasek's renaming, Parameswar was driven from the island. He did not go far. The former prince traveled north to Malacca on the Malayan Peninsula. He established a kingdom, eventually transforming Singapore into an outpost of his rule.

Another traveler from China may have seen Singapore before Wang Dayuan. Around 1292, Marco Polo began his return voyage to his home city of Venice, Italy after spending many years in China. Sailing through the South China Sea, he stayed for five months on the Indonesian island of Sumatra. Besides describing its landscape, unique animals, and people, he became probably the first European to explain what a monsoon was. As Polo described his trip to Sumatra, he noted that "It takes a full year to complete the voyage... for only two winds blow in these seas, one that wafts [blows] them out and one that brings them back."[1]

Polo and his crew left Sumatra when the monsoon winds changed direction. Traveling through the Strait of Malacca's narrow passage, he could have seen Singapore from the deck of his ship. If so, he would have been the first European to spot the island. He would not be the last.

Marco Polo (in green) may have been the first European to see the island which became known as Singapore. Here he, his father, and his uncle kneel before Chinese emperor Kublai Khan. Years later his adventures became a best-selling book.

Alfonso de Albuquerque (1453–1515) led the successful Portuguese attack against Malacca. One of the men under his command was Ferdinand Magellan, who later led the first expedition to sail around the world. This statue in de Albuquerque's honor is in Lisbon, Portugal.

The Europeans Arrive

Across Southeast Asia, a group of islands about 2,000 miles (3,200 kilometers) from Singapore known as the Moluccas became well-known for producing spices such as cinnamon, nutmeg, and pepper. These spices were shipped to eager buyers in Europe.

European countries like England, France and Spain competed for the fastest trade routes. Though it was smaller and less wealthy than those countries, Portugal took the lead. By the 1500s, Portuguese sailors had landed along both coasts of Africa, the Arabian Peninsula, and the East Indies. Portuguese ships sailed along the Strait of Malacca.

In 1511, Malacca, in present-day Malaysia, was attacked by Portuguese forces under the command of Alfonso de Albuquerque. The Malays fought back and their defense cost many Portuguese lives. The horrific battle was witnessed by Giovanni de Empoli, an Italian who fought with the Europeans and later described the locals as the "most valiant [brave] men, well-trained in war, and copiously supplied with every type of very good weapon."[1] The Malays' fearsome defense did not deter the Portuguese, however, as they eventually captured the city.

Afterward, Sultan Mahmud Shah—the ruler of the Malaccan kingdom—fled south. He established a new empire called Johor-Riau,

Commonplace today, nutmegs were once worth their weight in gold.

which extended to Singapore. That control ended in 1613, when Portuguese forces burned a trading post that had been established there.

However, Portugal was unable to maintain control of its far-flung properties. Their navy was no match for fleets from larger countries like Spain and the Netherlands. Singapore was often attacked by local forces, like the Johor-Riau and Sumatra's Aceh. In 1641, the Dutch drove Portugal out.

In 1795, the British took control of Malacca, although the Dutch ruled over the trade routes to China and the East Indies. The British East India Company (EIC) wanted to change that.

Taking risks and exploring unfamiliar lands may have been in Stamford Raffles's blood. His father was a merchant seaman. Raffles began working for the EIC as a clerk in London in 1795, when he was 14 years old. He began studying the Malay language and culture. He dreamed of traveling to the archipelago. Ten years later, his dream came true. He journeyed there and filled several key positions with the EIC.

Soon after his appointment in 1817 as governor-general of Bengkulu, an EIC post on Sumatra, Raffles had an idea which would change the future of Singapore. If Britain established a base somewhere along the southern tip of the Malay Peninsula, Raffles believed the country could control the strait. Since the fires set by the Portuguese more than two centuries earlier, Singapore had been virtually deserted. Yet Raffles saw an opportunity.

Later, Raffles would write, "But for my Malay Studies I should hardly have known that such a place existed; not only the European but the Indian world was ignorant of it. It is impossible to conceive a place combining more advantages. It is within a week's sail of China, still closer to Siam [Thailand]....in the very

This statue honors Sir Stamford Raffles, who left a permanent and indelible mark on Singapore.

FYI FACT:

Considered one of the best museums in Singapore, the Asian Civilizations Museum in the Empress Place Building offers exhibits on Southeast Asian history and the cultures which have influenced Singapore. Fine arts, furniture, and porcelain are among the displays in its galleries.

heart of the archipelago, or as the Malays call it, it is 'the navel of the Malay countries.'"[2]

The EIC decided the idea had merit. Raffles began negotiating with Singapore's temenggong Abdul Rahman, a senior minister for the Sultan of Johor. On February 6, 1819, Rahman signed a treaty with Raffles and the EIC. It allowed Britain to establish a trading post on Singapore in exchange for annual payments to the sultan.

Soon after, Raffles left Singapore, with Colonel William Farquhar in charge during his absence. When Raffles returned three years later, the island's development had exceeded his expectations. Merchants had arrived from Indonesia, China, and India with spices, coffee, gold dust, and exotic items like parrots and bird's nests that could be eaten. The population had nearly doubled. Yet in the midst of all the success, Raffles was stunned by the poverty he encountered. Workers lived in slums. Crime and disease were rampant. He set about redesigning Singapore. His plans not only changed the island in the 18th century. They helped it become a world power in the 21st.

Colonel William Farquhar managed Singapore after Raffles left. For three years he oversaw the island's growth but ignored the population's increasing poverty.

Located in the Kampong Glam Malay Heritage District, the Malay Heritage Center offers collections designed to honor Singapore's past while looking toward its future. It opened in 2004.

Raffles Neighborhoods

If Singapore has any national pastimes, most visitors and locals would agree, they are shopping and eating. Whether buying high-end clothing or bargain merchandise, dining at an inexpensive curry restaurant or enjoying an upscale five-course meal, the city is a consumer's paradise.

Strolling along Orchard Road, with its mile-long stretch of luxury retailers and high-end restaurants, visitors and residents alike can find it difficult to imagine Singapore's humble origins. Once a swampy backwater with deadly tigers and a small population, its sudden success challenged the island's colonial rulers.

Today Orchard Road might resemble New York City's Fifth Avenue, but in the early 1800s it was an area lined with nutmeg plantations and fruit orchards. Residential development arrived later than on other parts of the island. Shophouses replaced farmland. These combination home-businesses featured shops on the first floor while the owner and his family lived on the second.

Visitors from the United States can easily find familiar

In a country of malls and shops, the Orchard Road shopping center stands out for its variety of luxury stores, its design, and its sheer size.

FYI FACT:

Raffles also encouraged the construction of a school. The Singapore Institution was completed in 1835. In 1868, it was renamed Raffles Institution and primarily educated the sons of wealthy Chinese.

stores and restaurants but adventurous travelers seek out Singapore's ethnic enclaves. These neighborhoods offer an immersion in unfamiliar cultures. They owe their existence to one man: Stamford Raffles.

When Raffles returned to Singapore, he was dismayed. Today, the Singapore River neatly divides the city into Chinatown to the south and the Colonial District to the north. Back then, new arrivals from places like China, Arabia, Armenia, and India settled into rundown shacks along the river's banks.

During the year Raffles governed Singapore, he turned Forbidden Hill (now Fort Canning Hill) into his base. Another island hill would be leveled and eventually transformed into a commercial district bearing his name—Raffles Place.

The fast-growing city was crowded and dirty. The messy sprawl bothered Raffles. He created an alternative when he drew up the Town Plan of 1822. It designated ethnic areas called kampongs (or village sections) along with government and commercial districts.

Despite almost two centuries of development and modernization, the kampongs remain in existence. Not far from modern cars racing along Nicoll Highway, an ancient culture famous for its customs is nestled within the Kampong Glam Malay Heritage District. In the shadows of the Sultan Mosque (the island's largest Muslim worship center) lies Arab Street. Here Islamic faithful shop for halal—food prepared in accordance with Muslim dietary restrictions—side-by-side with non-Muslim Singaporeans and tourists drawn by the area's bargains.

Travel writer Jennifer Eveland often stops at Hadjee Textiles for sarongs. These long and colorful pieces of cloth are worn by men and women who either tuck it around their waist or under their arms. This traditional garment, Eveland says, is "perfect for traveling, as they're lightweight, but can serve you well as a dressy skirt, bed sheet, beach blanket, window shade, bath towel, or whatever you need—when I'm on the road, I can't live without mine."[1]

Besides sarongs, shoppers along Arab Street can find antiques, Southeast Asian handicrafts and tablecloths, and quilts from India. Like most shoppers familiar with local customs, Eveland notes that buying more than one item from a store lowers the prices. Haggling—negotiating a price with a shopkeeper—is a time-honored tradition in Singapore. Most locally owned stores encourage it, as do some hotels.

Observant Muslims are not allowed to come into contact with alcohol. They can't drink it and they can't wear it either. This eliminates most store-bought perfume. At Jamal Kazura Aromatics, shoppers buy oil-based, alcohol-free perfumes which imitate the scents of well-known

One of the most significant mosques in Singapore, the Sultan Mosque in the Kumpong Glam district is notable for its gleaming golden domes and its immense prayer hall. While the site dates back to 1824, the current structure was completed in 1928.

In the shadows of modernity, the shophouses along Serangoon Road line the main street through Singapore's Little India.

designers. Shoppers can even buy made-to-order perfume for a custom, one-of-a-kind scent.

Outside the shops, small stalls and stands offer a variety of local goods. Yet the Kampong Glam Malay Heritage District is just one example of Singapore's multi-cultural commerce. Arab Street's Maruti Textiles offers fabrics from India, and less than a mile away Little India offers an authentic Indian experience. Its crowded, chaotic streets and the pungent scent of curry seem a world away from the island's sterile business district. Little India preserves tradition for many residents who are far from home.

Along Serangoon Road, visitors delight in bright pastel buildings, colorful lights, and the expensive silks hanging from street stalls. With some of Little India's best shopping, Serangoon Road draws both bargain-hunting tourists and the country's many Indian residents. The street's biggest draw is the bustling Mustafa Centre.

Inside, shoppers enjoy a two-block long department store that never closes—it is open 24 hours a day! More modern than the area's smaller shops, it sells many of the same items that are found in malls the world over like sporting goods, digital cameras, and makeup. With a reputation for variety and reasonable prices, Mustafa Centre is very popular with Singaporeans.

What truly sets it apart are the authentic Indian goods. As Eveland notes, "the real finds are rows of saris, and silk fabrics; two floors of jaw-dropping gold jewelry in Indian designs; an entire supermarket packed with spices and packets of instant curries; ready-made Indian-style tie-dye and embroidered casual wear; incense and perfume oils; cotton tapestries and textiles for the home—the list goes on."[2]

Away from the noise of shoppers and shop-keepers, a moment of serenity can be enjoyed inside Little India's temples. The Sri Veeramakaliamman Temple is dedicated to the worship of the Hindu goddess Kali, who is celebrated for bringing about the death of the ego and ending self-centered thinking. The Sakaya Muni Buddha Gaya Temple is devoted to its namesake. Here a sitting Buddha is represented by a nearly 50-foot (15-meter) statue. Across Race Cross Road from the Sakaya Muni Temple (also known as the "Temple of 1000 Lights") is the Taoist Leong San Temple.

With its colorful statuary, the Sri Veeramakaliamman Hindu Temple attracts notice from both worshippers and casual visitors.

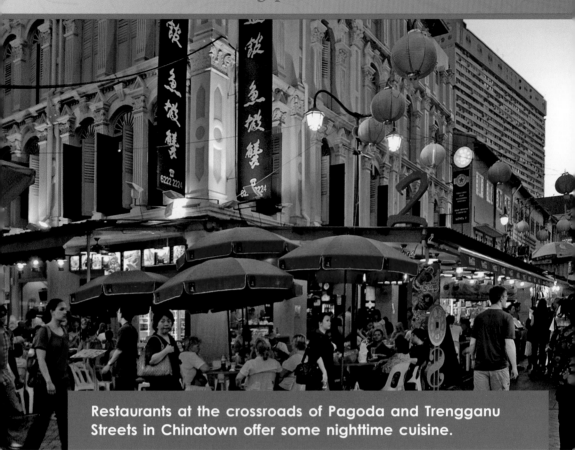

Restaurants at the crossroads of Pagoda and Trengganu Streets in Chinatown offer some nighttime cuisine.

Nearly 75 percent of Singaporeans are Chinese. Sprawling Chinatown reflects their influence. Located near Pearl's Hill City Park at the southeastern end of the city center, Chinatown overflows with small shops and restaurants which cater to travelers and native Chinese. Although many of the neighborhood's shophouses were torn down during the city's modernization in the 1960s and 1970s, today many have been lovingly renovated. Restored shophouses often sell for over $2 million.

Pagoda and Trengganu Streets are closed to cars. People stroll (and spend) freely along the boulevard where everything from Chinese silk robes to labor-intensive Vietnamese lacquerware is available for sale. Considered touristy by locals, the area's goods are often available for less money at the Chinatown complex further down Trengganu Street. For an escape from the noise and commerce, a pair of often-photographed temples dominate the Chinatown skyline.

Along Telok Ayer Street, the Thian Hock Keng Temple is the city's oldest Hokkien temple. Built in 1839, it reflects the traditional southern Chinese architectural style. Probably the most photographed landmark in Chinatown, however, is a temple with an Indian background—the Sri Mariamman Temple, the oldest Hindu temple in the city.

The city's well-preserved ethnic neighborhoods like Little India and Chinatown reflect Singapore's rich history of welcoming outsiders. By the early part of the 20th century, Singapore was often described as a success story. Yet the island was facing enormous challenges which threatened to eclipse its success.

The Thian Hock Keng Temple is the oldest Hokkien temple in Singapore. With its main temple dedicated to the Taoist goddess of the sea and its back temple honoring Buddha, the site attracts many of the city's faithful.

Rubber plants were smuggled out of Brazil to England in the 1850s. Several decades later, Henry Ridley of the Singapore Botanic Gardens acquired some samples. He figured out a method of growing them to meet a rising demand for rubber tires and raincoats. The region's supply of rubber fueled its growth.

The Rise
of Singapore

In the March 1926 issue of *National Geographic* magazine, a lengthy article on Singapore described the country's progress. "From a jungle isle, where tigers ate men at night, to a magnificent city, tenth among the ports of the world in less than a century!" declared one breathless sentence. "Through the thick jungle, where once led only the elephant paths, wide, level roads have now been built, and the hoarse squawk of the motor horn has drowned the fierce growls of the lurking tiger."[1]

More than one hundred years after Raffles returned to England (where he died penniless in 1826 at the age of 45), Singapore had become the jewel of the east. It had been built by thousands of immigrants and even prisoners. They arrived on its shores from halfway around the world. Many came to the "boom town" dreaming of a better life. Some died in its pursuit.

In 1824, under the Anglo-Dutch treaty, the Dutch withdrew their objections to British occupation of Singapore. In exchange for money and pensions, the sultan and the temenggong likewise relinquished control of the island. In 1826, it became part of the Straits Settlements, a British-controlled region which also included Malacca, Dinding, and Penang. In 1832, Singapore became the headquarters.

By the 1850s, Singapore trade had outgrown the Singapore River port. Shipping companies financed a larger port at New Harbor. The city attracted more than merchants and workers dreaming of wealth. Singapore also drew large waves of criminals who hoped to get rich. Like the pirates described by Wang Dayuan, this new generation of thieves attacked from boats. They rode out of the Philippines and China, assaulting merchant ships before escaping to island caves and coves. These 19th-century pirates were so bold that they stole from vessels docked in the harbor, then sold the goods openly along Singapore streets.

The Chinese arrived in the hundreds and thousands, quickly overwhelming the native Malays who had struggled on the island for centuries. Amongst Chinese immigrants, secret societies developed. These criminal organizations exploited new arrivals and encouraged downtown riots. Long before the American West, Singapore owned a reputation as a dangerous, lawless area where anything could be had for the right price. The island's small police force was overwhelmed.

Tin workers ladle molten metal from furnaces into molds to cool off. Tin production was low paying, but for those without work it represented opportunity.

FYI FACT:

Raffles began the city's first botanic garden in 1822 at Fort Canning, but it closed due to lack of funding seven years later.

In 1851, Thomas Dunman was appointed Singapore's first superintendent of police. His goal was to eliminate the lawless, reckless secret societies and reduce other criminal activities.

Even as he worked to end the violence of the secret societies and others, immigrant arrivals endured their own horrors.

Hoping for a better life in Singapore, they were secreted in ships and packed into cargo holds with little food or water. They became prey for the numerous fatal diseases which stalked so many in the 19th century. Once they arrived, many of them had to pay back the cost of their voyage—usually with at least a year's worth of work.

India also used Singapore as a penal colony, sending its prisoners to do the dangerous work of building bridges, constructing roads, and digging in mines. Many prisoners remained in Singapore after gaining their freedom, using the trade they'd learned to earn a living.

The opening of the Suez Canal in Egypt in 1869 linked the Mediterranean and Red Seas with South Asia, putting Singapore in a prime location for ships traveling between Europe and Asia. At about the same time, the rise of steamships made ports like Singapore less dependent on trade winds, even as they docked in the city's ports to refuel.

The Industrial Revolution transformed the island. This transition from handcrafted to machine-made goods shifted workers from farms to factories. It also fueled tremendous growth in entrepôt ports like Singapore. Mined in Malaya, tin was processed in Singaporean smelting plants, then shipped to factories across the world. By the 1900s, Singapore was the largest tin smelter in the world.

Another source of prosperity came from the first director of the Singapore Botanic Gardens, English botanist Henry Ridley. He became famous for smuggling rubber plants into Singapore. He worked tirelessly to convince neighboring Malay farmers to grow them. His work earned

General Tomoyuki Yamashita became known as the "Tiger of Malaya" for his brilliant leadership of invading Japanese forces who captured Malaya and Singapore. He later commanded the defense of the Philippines. Charged with war crimes, he was convicted in a controversial decision and executed in 1946.

him nicknames like "Mad" and "Rubber" Ridley. Ridley began experimenting with different methods of growing rubber plants and extracting their latex without harming the plants. After disease devastated Malay coffee plantations, the farmers finally gave Ridley's rubber plants a try. They were an immediate success.

In an effort to modernize Singapore's port, the Singapore Harbor Board constructed two large docks in 1917. Britain also developed military bases in and around Singapore, building a large naval station and several airfields.

By the 1920s, Singapore was benefitting enormously from the growing automobile industry. In the United States, Ford Motor Company founder Henry Ford designed an assembly line to speed the production of cars and make them less expensive and therefore more affordable for the average person. Throughout the decade, wages grew while income taxes declined. This helped develop a vibrant Western economy where more people bought cars and other consumer products, many of which relied on metals and rubber processed in Singapore.

Everything changed on October 29, 1929. The U.S. stock market crashed, which began what would be known as The Great Depression. It devastated Singapore. Factories shut down. Port business declined. Fewer workers were needed. For the first time the region stopped welcoming immigrants. Instead, thousands of people from India and China were forced to return home.

In 1931, Japanese forces invaded Manchuria, a Chinese territory. In Singapore, many of the remaining young Chinese men returned home to fight. Others refused to buy Japanese goods.

Despite the Great Depression and increasing hostility from Japan, Singaporeans, European nationals, and other island inhabitants believed better times were just around the corner. They were wrong.

On December 7, 1941, Japanese forces attacked the U.S. naval base at Pearl Harbor, Hawaii. At virtually the same time, Japan attacked military installations on the Philippines and dropped bombs on Singapore. Japanese troops also landed in southern Thailand and northern Malaya.

Singapore was well-protected from the water side. It was ill-prepared for an invasion from the landward side. Japanese soldiers—many of them riding bicycles—easily moved south through Malaya. On February 8, 1942 they began attacking Singapore, using small boats to cross the narrow channel to the island.

Tomoyuki Yamashita, the Japanese general in charge of the attack, wasn't sure he would win. "My attack on Singapore was a bluff, a bluff that worked," he explained. "I had 30,000 men and was outnumbered more than three to one. I knew if I had to fight long for Singapore I would be beaten. That is why the surrender had to be at once. I was very frightened all the time that the British would discover our numerical weakness and lack of supplies and force me into disastrous street fighting."[1]

The bluff worked. The British surrendered a week later. Life in Singapore became extraordinarily difficult. The Japanese harassed, arrested, and tortured many people, especially the Chinese. The invaders also executed anyone they suspected of helping the British.

In August 1945, Japan surrendered. British forces soon returned to Singapore. Their return did not end the hardships. Prices rose and food was scarce. These conditions led to labor actions like strikes, with workers walking off their jobs in protest.

Newly formed political groups demanded better treatment for workers and independence for Singapore. Both the Singapore Labour Party and the Singapore Progressive Party claimed they could achieve these goals, but the People's Action Party (PAP) succeeded. Founded by Singapore lawyer Lee Kuan Yew in 1954, it became the winning party in the 1959 elections. That year, Yew was elected prime minister of Singapore. It was allowed internal self-government but the British remained in control of defense and foreign affairs.

In September 1963, Singapore joined the Federation of Malaysia. Most Singaporeans, including Yew, believed their survival depended upon this union. Unfortunately, the two countries often had disputes over economic and political issues. Malaysia was also concerned that while most Malaysians were Malay, the majority of Singaporeans—including Yew—had Chinese origins. When the PAP became active in

The United States and Singapore have forged significant political and economic ties. U.S. Secretary of Defense William S. Cohen meets with Singapore Ambassador Chan Heng Chee (left) and former Prime Minister Lee Kuan Yew in 2000.

Malaysia, the country asked Singapore to exit the federation. On August 9th, 1965, Yew went on national television to announce that Singapore was completely independent. This was not a joyous occasion. Indeed, Yew began to cry as he made his announcement. Like most people then, he did not believe his tiny island nation could survive on its own.

The Chinese New Year attracts crowds of every ethnicity. One of the most popular parts of the celebration is the Chingay Parade. It originated in 1973 to replace a ban on firecrackers and features decorated floats, acrobats, dances, and more.

Celebrate!

Although modern Singapore is a diverse nation of many cultures, the country's main ethnic groups have many things in common. Chinese, Indian, and Malay cultures all celebrate the strength of family and the value of worship. Chinese are predominantly Tao or Buddhist. Buddhism's core belief is that happiness can only be achieved by eliminating desire. Tao is focused on balance. Most Indians in Singapore practice Hinduism, a belief system more than 3,000 years old. Many of Singapore's Malays are Muslims who follow the teachings of the Prophet Muhammad, while Christianity has been practiced since the arrival of the British in the 1800s.

Freedom of religion is guaranteed by Singapore's constitution. Although Jehovah's Witnesses were banned in 1972 (because their members avoided the country's required military service), not only are most religions welcomed in Singapore, but also all of the country's main religions are included amongst the country's ten national holidays.

FYI FACT:

Christians compose less than 15 percent of the population of Singapore. Many worship at one of the three churches built by British colonials: the Armenian Church, Saint Andrew's Cathedral, and Singapore's first permanent Catholic Church, the Cathedral of the Good Shepherd.

Singaporeans also celebrate the traditional New Year's Eve on December 31st and mark the occasion with fireworks displays.

The first holiday of the year—New Year's Day—includes everyone. New Year's Eve is celebrated with fireworks over the city's Marina Bay while New Year's Day is welcomed with worship services and buffets at most major hotels.

For the city's many Chinese residents, the New Year doesn't begin until the Chinese New Year. This celebration marks the beginning of the lunar New Year. It arrives each year in late January to early February with parades of stilt walkers, lion dancers, and floats along Orchard Road. Chinese families celebrate by giving children red envelopes stuffed with money while forgiving those who owe them.

In January, two Hindu celebrations take place. One is the feast of Pongal (which means "overflow" in Tamil). This festival is celebrated with food offerings like sugar, rice, and milk at the Sri Srinvasa Perumal Temple. The other, the Thaipusam, is more of a visual feast. Visitors and Hindus alike can watch the Hindu faithful who parade outside of the temple with complex steel arches piercing their skin. Some even pierce their tongues and cheeks with hooks which are hung with fruit.

The main Buddhist holiday, Vesak Day, honors Buddha's birth, and falls on the full moon in the month of Vesakha (April/May). The faithful chant prayers at Buddhist temples, perform acts of kindness, and release caged birds in celebration.

The summer offers a variety of entertainments. In July, the Dragon Boat Festival features boats with 22 paddlers from all over the world. Their boats are decorated by a dragon's head and tail. They compete in races honoring Chinese scholar Qu Yuan, who drowned himself to protest political corruption. August 9th is Singapore National Day. On this holiday, the country's independence is celebrated with a huge show at the National Stadium that features military parades and fireworks.

August (and sometimes September) also features the Chinese Festival of the Hungry Ghosts. Red candles and paper money are burned outside of Chinese homes to appease the souls of the dead released from purgatory during the seventh lunar month.

Late September/early October brings another painful holiday with the Birthday of the Monkey God. Celebrated by Singapore's Taoists, the day honors the Monkey God, who managed to sneak into heaven and gain magical powers. He is believed to cure the sick. Taoist monks honor him by going into a trance during which they are entered by his spirit. They then howl and cut themselves with knives. Puppet shows and Chinese operas are also performed.

Late in the year, in November or December, Muslims celebrate Hari Ray Haji. This honors one of the five pillars of Islam, making the hajj—the required once-in-a-lifetime journey to the Saudi Arabian city of Mecca. After making the trip, Muslim men have the title of Haji while Muslim women earn the title of Hajjah. Following morning prayers on this holiday—which takes place on the last day of the hajj—goats and sheep are sacrificed with the meat given to the poor. It serves as a reminder for the faithful to share their wealth.

Christians in Singapore celebrate Christmas on December 25th. Much of the city celebrates the holiday with traditional songs, while many of the city's malls are decorated with festive lights which have been put up several weeks earlier.

Dragon boat races are one facet of World Water Day, celebrated in March. It also includes bike races and environmental activities. The objective is to focus on the importance of fresh water.

Singaporean international star Nadya Hutagalung arrives at a closing day event for ScreenSingapore 2011 alongside her husband Desmond Koh. Koh is a former competitive swimmer who represented Singapore in three Olympics. The couple have three children.

Singapore People to Know

Singapore has many talented and famous people. Here are just a few.

Lee Kuan Yew (1923–) Perhaps no one is as responsible for modern Singapore as Lee, who was nearly executed by the Japanese during World War II. After the war, he received his education at England's Cambridge University. He entered politics soon after returning to Singapore in 1949. Five years later he formed the People's Action Party (PAP), which won the 1959 elections. Lee became prime minister, a position he continued to hold until he stepped down in 1990. Because of his importance to the nation, a special position called Minister Mentor of Singapore was created for him in 2004. It was abolished when he retired from politics seven years later. Many people still refer to him as the "Father of Singapore," or more familiarly by his initials LKY.

Richard "Dick" Lee Peng Boon (1956–) From his first album in 1974, this Singaporean singer has championed Asian elements in pop music.

Dick Lee is a composer, a playwright, and a pop singer. He also has a strong interest in fashion and served as creative director for Singapore's National Day Parade.

After a stint living in Japan, Boon—also a playwright and composer—wrote an autobiography called *Adventures of a Mad Chinaman* and developed magazines and musicals. He also was noted for serving as the critical—even insulting—judge for several seasons on *Singapore Idol*, when he sometimes told auditioning talent to get singing lessons.

Nadya Hutagalung (1974–) When Hutagalung was a girl, "her mother regaled her with stories about rescuing Orang Utans stolen from an Indonesian zoo, and filled her mind with phrases that would only become part of the global lexicon much later, like 'living off the grid' and being 'self sustainable,'" according to Fly Entertainment. "It sparked a lifetime of loving nature, rescuing strays and truly appreciating what we as humans take from the earth."[1] Although well-known as one of the first video jockeys on MTV Asia and as a VJ on MTV USA, Hutagalung has focused much of her energy on "Green Kampong," which promotes environmental education and conservation. She is ambassador of the World Wildlife Fund's Earth Hour in Singapore. She is also a host of *Asia's Next Top Model* TV show and was named one of Singapore's 20 most influential people in 2009 by the Cable News Network.

Dr. Lee Wei Ling (1955–) Yew's daughter runs the National Neuroscience Institute. She also is an accomplished writer, whose articles on a wide variety of aspects of life in Singapore appear in many media outlets. She is especially noted for her simple lifestyle. She and her parents live in the same house the family has had since 1945 even though their accomplishments would have allowed them to move into a much larger and more lavish dwelling. In an article published in 2013, she commented that "When the end approaches and we look back on our lives, will we regret the latest mobile phone or luxury car that we did not acquire? Or would we prefer to die at peace with ourselves, knowing that we have lived lives filled with love, friendship and goodwill, that we have helped some of our fellow voyagers along the way and that we have tried our best to leave this world a slightly better place than how we found it? We know which the correct choice is—and it is within our power to make that choice."[2]

Lee Hsien Loong (1952–) The son of Lee Kuan Yew, Lee received a masters degree from Harvard University in 1980. He also served for 12 years in the Singapore Armed Forces, becoming its youngest-ever

LEE HSIEN-

At a session covering the Outlook for East Asia at the 2012 annual meeting of the World Economic Forum, Singapore's Prime Minister Lee Hsien Loong offers his views.

brigadier general in 1983. He entered politics soon afterward and served as deputy prime minister from 1990 to 2004. He was elected as prime minister in 2004, and re-elected in 2011. During his time in office he has reduced state control of the private sector and cut the work week to five days, eliminating the Saturday half-day that had been common up to that time.

Min Lee (1982–) A violinist from the age of two, she gave her first public performance three years later. She came to the United States when she was nine to study music and began attending Yale University at the age of 14. Since then Lee has performed with such notable groups as the Royal Philharmonic and the Vienna Chamber Orchestra along with the Singapore Symphony Orchestra. She has also helped raise millions of dollars for charity.

Edwin Thumboo (1933–) The son of an Indian schoolteacher and a Chinese homemaker, Thumboo began writing poetry when he was 17. Since then, the Singapore writer and critic has produced several critically acclaimed books of poetry in English: *Rib of Earth* (1954, while he was still a university student), *Gods Can Die* (1977), *Ulysses by the*

Min Lee has been performing since she was a toddler. Today she is a popular concert violinist, nicknamed "Singapore's poster girl of classical music."

Merlion (1979), and *A Third Map* (1993). Because his work focuses on the history and culture of the country, many people consider him as Singapore's poet laureate. He has also written a two-volume set of nursery rhymes, *Child's Delight*.

Goh Chok Tong (1941–) A competitive swimmer as a youth, Goh was educated at the Raffles Institution and the University of Singapore. He received a masters degree from Williams College in Williamstown, Massachusetts in 1967. He returned to Singapore, where he soon became managing director of Neptune Orient Lines and played a key role in the company's growth. He entered politics in 1976 and become the second prime minister of Singapore when he succeeded Lee Kuan Yew in 1990. He served until 2004. As an indication of the esteem in which he is held internationally, he was a candidate for the position of United Nations Secretary-General in 2006. However, Ban Ki-moon of Korea was eventually selected. Goh remains active in Singaporean civic and cultural affairs.

Singapore is preparing for success in the 21st century by maintaining strong ties with its neighbors. Here former Prime Minister Goh Chok Tong (right) shakes hands with China's Vice Premier Zhang Gaoli during a meeting on October 22, 2013.

Once a nation of rundown shacks and houses, Singapore today is filled with skyscrapers like these in Bukit Batok. Bukit Batok is a "new town," which means it was carefully planned from its beginnings in 1979.

Singapore Today

Singapore is more than just a successful port. It's an island filled with successful people. There are more millionaires per capita in Singapore than anywhere else in the world. Even public servants like government administrators earn large salaries. As *Wall Street Journal* writer Shibani Mahtani observes, "Looking for millionaires? Take a drive around Singapore's residential districts—more than one in six houses you see will be inhabited by one....Singapore had 188,000 millionaire households in 2011—or slightly more than 17% of its resident households."[1]

Not only are so many Singaporeans wealthy, they built their fortunes in a hurry. As Malminderjit Singh of *The Business Times* points out, "If you are looking to getting rich quickly then being in Singapore is your best bet to do so....The latest report in the Barclays Wealth Insights series shows the wealthy in Singapore took the least time to build their riches, with more than half of them, or 51 percent, doing it in less than 10 years."[2]

In the beginning—when the country split off from Malaysia—even Lee Kuan Yew had his doubts about the chances of his country's ultimate success. "I had to make it work or we'd all die," he told author Dan Buettner. "This little island with no resources had to survive.... We had to be of relevance to the world. That relevance was economics: Our efficiency, our ability to provide a base for secure production, commerce services...transportation of people and goods, in every possible way."[3]

FYI FACT:

In 1994, American student Michael Fay was sentenced to a six-stroke caning for vandalism. Despite protests from U.S. President Bill Clinton, the sentence was carried out.

Lee believes most outsiders failed to notice Singapore's best feature. "We had the advantage first of an immigrant population," he explained to Buettner. "They have left their secure moorings—China, India, Indonesia—and they have come here to make good. So they are more willing to change than people in their own countries."[4]

And change they did. As prime minister, Lee led a government which demanded extraordinary changes from its people. The choices he made helped ensure his nation's survival. Some say they also severely limited people's freedom.

In the 1960s, the country was a land of contrasts. Very rich people lived in lavish homes while the poor struggled to survive and went home to decaying shacks. The government created the Housing and Development Board. Under its leadership, numerous homes, whether they were in disrepair or not, were torn down in the 1960s and 1970s and replaced by high-rises. These large apartment buildings are subsidized, or partly paid for, by the government. Today 85 percent of the country's population lives in one of these homes.

As the city expanded beyond its original borders, there was very little land available for those who wished to live in a non-government home. This makes them expensive—a 500-square-foot (46 square meters) studio condo can cost over one million dollars.

Yew inherited a landscape altered by over a century of development. Long before most cities in the U.S. required residential and commercial developers to set aside land for parks, Singapore in the 1960s made sure that parks were created alongside high-rises.

Although Singapore's air quality has improved, it is often polluted by nearby countries with fewer restrictions. Forest fires in Indonesia deliberately set by logging and plantation companies have blown smoke across Singapore, causing extraordinary levels of pollution.

In Singapore, only the very well-off can afford to drive. The rest use public transportation, like this Singapore Municipal Rapid Transit train.

This is one reason why the government has promoted public transit. In 1990 the first two lines of Singapore Mass Rapid Transit opened. Today the SMRT trains offer regular stops, with most trains arriving every six minutes during peak travel times.

To increase the appeal of public transit, the government makes owning a car very expensive. Buying a car in Singapore means paying extraordinarily high taxes. Because of these taxes, relatively few Singaporeans own their own cars. "I'm having second thoughts about buying a car," said Stephan Ritzmann, a Swiss executive at a local luxury watch retailer who moved to Singapore not long ago. "In Switzerland, cars cost less than half of what they cost here. The government wants us to use public transport and it works pretty well."[5]

After Singapore's independence, the government also became more involved with schooling. It began setting educational standards. The city was predominantly Chinese. Many in this community, including the Chinese Chamber of Commerce, believed Chinese should be the national language. Lee refused.

He'd seen how Malaysia had suffered by making Malay its national language. He wanted his people fluent in a language that was widely spoken, especially by people in the wealthy countries he hoped would conduct business in Singapore. He also did not want to select the first language of most Singaporeans. So he chose the language spoken by the country's colonial rulers.

"We decided to keep English and also teach each group's mother tongue—Chinese, Mandarin, Malay, whatever," he explained. "That gave us an enormous advantage."[6]

Having all children learn one common language, regardless of their race or ethnic background, did more than help them prepare for jobs.

It also forged a national identity. Today it doesn't matter where a person comes from. Anyone who attends school in Singapore speaks English along with their native language. Today half of Singaporeans are literate—able to read and write—in two languages.

This was one more way Singaporeans prepared for the 21st century. An educated, English-speaking workforce and a very low rate of taxation to foreign businesses and their workers have helped Singapore attract a number of companies that set up manufacturing plants and corporate headquarters.

In addition to adopting English, Singapore also adopted the government structure of its one-time colonial administrator. Both Singapore and Great Britain have a parliament and a prime minister. In Singapore, 87 members of Parliament are elected by the people. Up to a dozen more are chosen by a select parliamentary committee. The prime minister is responsible for the country's operations while the president is the head of state and chooses the prime minister.

Although there were candidates from other political parties, between 1968 and 1981 there was not a single non-PAP member of Parliament. PAP has held the majority of the Parliament seats since then. PAP has always won both the presidency and a party member has been prime minister. The most public face of the new Singapore, PAP founder Lee, remained prime minister for over 30 years. When he stepped down in 1990, he was succeeded by deputy prime minister Goh Chok Tong.

Elections in Singapore don't always happen as scheduled. In 1999 the Elections Committee disqualified every presidential candidate except Singapore's former ambassador to the United States, S.R. Nathan. The election was cancelled and Nathan became president. In 2005, the committee again disqualified everyone except Nathan and he became president again. The year before, Lee's son, Lee Hsien Loong, became prime minister.

Even if they are presented with very few choices, eligible voters are expected to cast a ballot. Not voting can get a person fined. So can many other things. "Singapore is a fine city" is a sort of unofficial city slogan. It means it is not only a pleasant place but also that numerous behaviors will earn a fine.

Buying or selling gum is illegal. So is spitting or smoking in public. Serious crimes, like drug dealing or possession, are punished by death. People convicted of less serious crimes like vandalism are beaten with a thin rattan cane—usually severely enough to break the skin.

As the prime minister for over three decades, Lee maintained tight control of his country. Unlike the United States, freedom of the press does not exist in Singapore. News stories must be approved by government officials. They are censored, or cut out, if the government dislikes them. It is illegal for someone in Singapore to connect a TV to a satellite dish because it could pick up transmissions from outside of the country. The Internet is carefully regulated and many popular websites are unavailable.

Lee is unapologetic. He believes the laws of his country have helped it become one of the safest cities in the world, a place where most people feel comfortable walking home alone after dark. The laws against bribery and fraud also have helped Singapore earn a top spot among the least corrupt countries in the world.

Despite the planning and organization, even Singapore has endured economic challenges. For decades, the country had a growth rate of 7 to 9 percent (the United States considers 3 percent to be good; it has averaged less than 1 percent since 2008). In 2003, travel to Southeast Asia was greatly reduced because of an outbreak of severe acute respiratory syndrome (SARS). This disease was highly contagious and sometimes fatal. The nation's economy contracted by more than 11 percent.

The global economic crisis of 2008–2009, like the Great Depression, had a huge impact on Singapore. The country's growth again declined, dropping as much as 5 percent. The government provided a multi-billion-dollar stimulus package. New casinos and international theme parks, along with a redeveloped marina, were built to attract more visitors.

Despite these and other challenges, Singapore faces the new millennium's second decade uniquely well-prepared to continue its success story.

Chili Crab

One of the most recognizable dishes in Singapore is chili crab. It's a fairly easy, if not inexpensive dish. It is very spicy. You will want an adult's help as this recipe involves hot oil.

Ingredients:
2 Dungeness crabs
5 tablespoons ketchup
1 cup water
2 tablespoons cornstarch
¾ teaspoon dark soy sauce
5 tablespoons vegetable oil
7 cloves garlic, crushed
2 tablespoons chopped shallots (onions)
10 red chili peppers, pounded with seeds
¾ teaspoon lemon juice
1 egg, beaten
4 green onions, minced

Preparation:
Prepare the following recipe with adult supervision:
1. Wash the crabs, then separate the claws. After cracking the shell, cut the body into pieces.
2. Combine ketchup, water, cornstarch, and soy sauce in a large bowl.
3. Heat the oil in a skillet, then stir in garlic and shallots. Fry for one to two minutes before adding the chili. After frying for another two minutes, add the crabs. Fry for about two minutes.
4. Add the sauce mixture to the crabs, coating them well.
   Cover and simmer on high heat for seven minutes. The crabs should be bright red.
5. Remove cover, stir in lime juice and then the beaten egg until it is cooked. Stir in the green onions. Enjoy.

Singapore Sarong

Singapore is an island nation with numerous cultures. There are few crafts that can be considered "Singaporean." The sarong is a symbol of Malaysia and is often worn by non-Malays. It is fairly easy to make.

Materials
- A colorful and lightweight fabric
- Fabric tape measure
- Straight pins
- Pencil
- Iron
- Thread
- Sewing machine or needle

Instructions
1. Determine the size of sarong you will need. The average size is 72 inches (183 centimeters) long by 40 inches (102 cm) wide for an adult; most children's sizes are 36 inches (92 cm) x 20 inches (51 cm).
2. At a local fabric store, select lightweight fabrics like woven cotton, charmeuse, and silk chiffon in pleasing colors. Ask them to cut the fabric slightly larger than the sizes suggested above. It is always better to buy more than you need. Make sure to wrap the fabric around you to ensure a proper fit.
3. With a fabric tape measure, measure the width and length of the sarong. Mark the measurements with straight pins, then cut along the pins. When you have completed cutting, you should have a large rectangle.
4. You can leave the edge as a fringe or hem the cut edges of the sarong by folding each edge over by about 1/4 of an inch (.65 cm). Use the iron to press the folds flat. Sew the inside edge using the sewing machine or a needle and thread (use a thread color which matches the fabric).
5. Try on the sarong and practice tying it. Tying sarongs can be tricky.

TIMELINE

Dates CE

1290s	Marco Polo, on his return trip to Venice after years in China, spends time on the island of Sumatra and may have seen Singapore.
1300s	By now, Singapore is called "Temasek," or "place surrounded by water" and has become a trading center.
1349	Wang Dayuan writes about his visit to the island.
1390	Sumatran Prince Parameswara invades the island and renames it Singapura, which means "lion city" in Sanskrit.
1613	Singapore is destroyed by Portuguese attacks.
1819	Representing the British East India Trading Company, Sir Stamford Raffles reaches an agreement to establish a trading post on the island.
1822	Raffles draws up a plan for Singapore that establishes kampongs or village sections for different ethnic groups.
1826	Singapore becomes one of four British territories in the Straits Settlements.
1832	Singapore becomes the capital of the Straits Settlements.
1850s	Shipping companies build facilities at New Harbor along Singapore's southern coast.
1859	The Singapore Botanic Gardens is founded.
1869	Completion of the Suez Canal increases the importance of Singapore as a port.
1922	Singapore becomes the most important British naval base in East Asia.
1942	Japan captures Singapore during World War II.
1945	After Japan is defeated, the British resume control of Singapore.
1959	Lee Kuan Yew becomes prime minister.
1963	Singapore joins the Federation of Malaysia.
1965	Singapore leaves the Federation of Malaysia and becomes an independent country.
1971	The final British forces leave Singapore.
1990	Prime Minister Lee Kuan Yew stands down after 31 years in office; Goh Chok Tong becomes the new prime minister.
1993	Ong Teng Cheong becomes the first elected president of Singapore.
1998	Singapore falls into a recession, the first in 13 years.
1999	S.R. Nathan becomes president in an uncontested election.
2001	First anti-government legal demonstration outside of election campaign.
2002	Japan and Singapore sign a free trade agreement.

2003	An outbreak of the SARS virus becomes a major health crisis.
2004	Lee Kuan Yew's son Lee Hsien Loong becomes prime minister.
2005	The government approves a plan to legalize casino gambling and build two multibillion-dollar casinos.
2009	Singapore begins to recover from its worst-ever recession.
2011	Tony Tan is narrowly elected president; Lee Hsien Loong wins re-election as prime minister.
2014	Prime Minister Lee Hsien Loong welcomed the growing cooperation between Singapore and Malaysia, and looks forward to the further deepening of their bilateral ties.

CHAPTER NOTES

Chapter 1: Singapore Overview
1. Gretchen Liu, *Singapore: A Pictorial History 1819–2000* (Oxford, United Kingdom: Routledge, 2011), p. 79.
2. Tan Dawn Wei, "This could be Singapore's first World Heritage Site," *Straits Times*, April 1, 2013. http://wildsingaporenews.blogspot.com/2013/04/this-could-be-singapores-first-world.html?utm_source=feedburner&utm_medium=feed&utm_campaign=Feed%3A+WildsingaporeNews+%28wildsingapore+news%29&utm_content=Google+Reader#.Uf1Tim26gct

Chapter 2: Early Visitors
1. Denis Belliveau and Francis Donnell, *In the Footsteps of Marco Polo* (Lanham, Maryland: Rowman & Littlefield, 2008), p. 209.

Chapter 3: Europeans Arrive
1. Nicholas Tarling (editor), I*nteraction and Adaptation, The Cambridge History of Southeast Asia* (Cambridge, United Kingdom: Cambridge University Press, 2008), p. 41.
2. "Singapore," The Chautauquan, Vol. 12. Original from Princeton University, M. Bailey Publisher, 1891. Digitized April 17, 2008, p. 742.

Chapter 4: Raffles Neighborhoods
1. Jennifer Eveland, "Singapore Shopping," *Frommer's Singapore & Malaysia*. 7th ed. (Hoboken, New Jersey, Wiley Publishing, 2011), p. 169.
2. Ibid., p. 170.

Chapter 5: The Rise of Singapore
1. Frederick Simpich, "Singapore: Crossroads of the East." *National Geographic*, March 1926, pp. 237–238.
2. "Yamashita's Bluff," Britain at War. http://www.britain-at-war.org.uk/WW2/Malaya_and_Singapore/html/body_yamashitas_bluff.htm

Chapter 7: Singapore People to Know

1. "Female Artistes: Nadya Hutagalung," Fly Entertainment. http://www.fly.com.sg/index.php/things-we-do/artiste-management/female-artistes/71-nadya-hutagalung
2. Lee Wei Ling, "My house is shabby, but it is comfortable," January 4, 2009, *The Sunday Times.* http://chemgen.wordpress.com/2009/01/05/who-is-lee-wei-ling/

Chapter 8: Singapore Today

1. Shibani Mahtani, "Singapore No. 1 For Millionaires—Again." *The Wall Street Journal/Southeast Asia*, June 1, 2012. http://blogs.wsj.com/searealtime/2012/06/01/singapore-no-1-for-millionaires-again/
2. Malminderjit Singh, "Singapore is world's most fertile land for millionaires." *The Business Times*, July 4, 2013. http://news.asiaone.com/News/Latest+News/Plush/Story/A1Story20130703-434349.html
3. Dan Buettner, *Thrive: Finding Happiness the Blue Zones Way* (Washington, D.C.: National Geographic, 2010), pp. 100–101.
4. Ibid., p. 112.
5. Kristine Aquino, "BMW Costing $260,000 Means Cars Only for Rich in Singapore as Taxes Climb." Bloomberg.com, February 16, 2011. http://www.bloomberg.com/news/2011-02-16/bmw-3-series-costs-260-000-as-singapore-tax-keeps-cars-for-rich.html
6. Buettner, *Thrive*, p. 102.

FURTHER READING

Books

Barber, Nicola. *Singapore* (Great Cities of the World). Milwaukee, Wisconsin: World Almanac Books, 2005.

Blocksidge, David, and Ingo Jezierski. *Exciting Singapore A Visual Journey*. Hong Kong: Tuttle Publishing, 2012.

Kummer, Patricia K. *Singapore*. New York: Children's Press, 2003.

Layton, Lesley, and Guek Pang. *Singapore*. Tarrytown, New York: Marshall Cavendish, 2012.

Lin, Yong Jui, and James Michael Baker. *Welcome to Singapore* (Welcome to My Country). Milwaukee, Wisconsin: Gareth Stevens, 2003.

On the Internet

Arab Street Photos
  http://www.youtube.com/watch?v=9S8eub31ve4
Singapore Botanic Gardens
  http://www.sbg.org.sg
Singapore Food
  http://www.makantime.com/
Singapore Parks Guide
  http://www.nparks.gov.sg/cms/

Books

Belliveau, Denis, and Francis Donnell. *In the Footsteps of Marco Polo*. Lanham, Maryland: Rowman & Littlefield Publishers, 2008.

Buettner, Dan. *Thrive: Finding Happiness the Blue Zones Way*. Washington, D.C.: National Geographic, 2010.

The Chautauquan, Vol. 12. Original from Princeton University, M.Bailey Publisher, 1891. Digitized April 17, 2008. p. 742.

de Ledesma, Charles. *The Rough Guide to Malaysia, Singapore and Brunei*. New York: Rough Guides, 2006.

Eveland, Jennifer. *Frommer's Singapore & Malaysia*. Hoboken, New Jersey: Wiley Publishing, 2011.

Heidhues, Mary F. *Southeast Asia: A Concise History*. New York: Thames & Hudson, 2000.

Liu, Gretchen. *Singapore: A Pictorial History 1819–2000*. Oxford, United Kingdom: Routledge, 2011.

Oakley, Matt. *Singapore*. 7th ed. Footscray, Australia: Lonely Planet, 2006.

Tarling, Nicholas (editor). *The Cambridge History of Southeast Asia*. Cambridge, United Kingdom: Cambridge University Press, 2008.

Wallace, Alfred Russel. *The Malay Archipelago, the land of the orang-utan and the bird of paradise*. London: Macmillan, 1869. (Project Gutenberg e-book edition: The Malay Archipelago: Volume I, 2008, Rev. 2013) http://www.gutenberg.org/files/2530/2530-h/2530-h.htm#2HCH0001.

Williams, China. *Southeast Asia on a Shoestring*. Footscray, Australia: Lonely Planet, 2010.

Periodicals

Kolesnikov-Jessop, Sonia. "In Singapore, a Renovated Shop House," *New York Times*, February 3, 2009. http://www.nytimes.com/2009/02/04/greathomesanddestinations/04gh-singapore.html?_r=0

Kristof, Nicholas D. "Big Brother," *The New York Times*, November 5, 2000. http://www.nytimes.com/books/00/11/05/reviews/001105.05kristot.html.

Simpich, Frederick. "Singapore, Crossroads of the East," *National Geographic*, March, 1926.

Suddath, Claire. "The Crash of 1929." *Time*, Oct 29, 2008. http://www.time.com/time/nation/article/0,8599,1854569,00.html.

On the Internet

BBC—Singapore Timeline
http://www.bbc.co.uk/news/world-asia-15971013

Botanic Gardens History
http://www.sbg.org.sg/aboutus/ourhistory.asp

Orchard Road
http://www.orchardroad.org/

Singapore History
http://www.focussingapore.com/information-singapore/history.html

Singapore People: "The Singapore Hot List: 20 People to Watch."
http://travel.cnn.com/singapore/none/singapore-hot-list-20-people-watch-759894

Singapore Recipe
http://allrecipes.com/recipe/singaporean-chile-crab/

GLOSSARY

charmeuse (SHAHR-myooz)—Soft fabric made of silk or synthetic materials, with a satin face and dull back.

dim sum (DIHM SUHM)—Chinese dish of steamed or fried dumplings with a variety of fillings; either a snack or main course.

eradicated (uh-RAA-dih-cay-tuhd)—Eliminated, destroyed.

fossils (FAW-suhlz)—The remains of a living creature preserved in the earth's crust.

halal (huh-LAHL)—Food specially prepared according to Islamic law and free from pork, which Muslims may not eat.

junks (JUHNKS)—Flat-bottomed Chinese ships with raised sterns and wide sails.

latex (LAY-teks)—Milky white fluid that is the source of natural rubber.

per capita (PUHR CAA-puh-tuh)—Literally "by the head"; per person or unit of population.

poet laureate (POH-uht LAWR-ee-uht)—Poet honored for his or her excellence and/or representing a group or a nation.

proximity (PRAWK-sih-muh-tee)—Closeness in space, in time, or in a relationship.

rattan (raa-TAN)—Thin, pliable palm stems.

saris (SAW-rees)—Indian women's garments consisting of a long silk or cotton cloth wrapped around the body with one end draped over one shoulder or the head.

INDEX

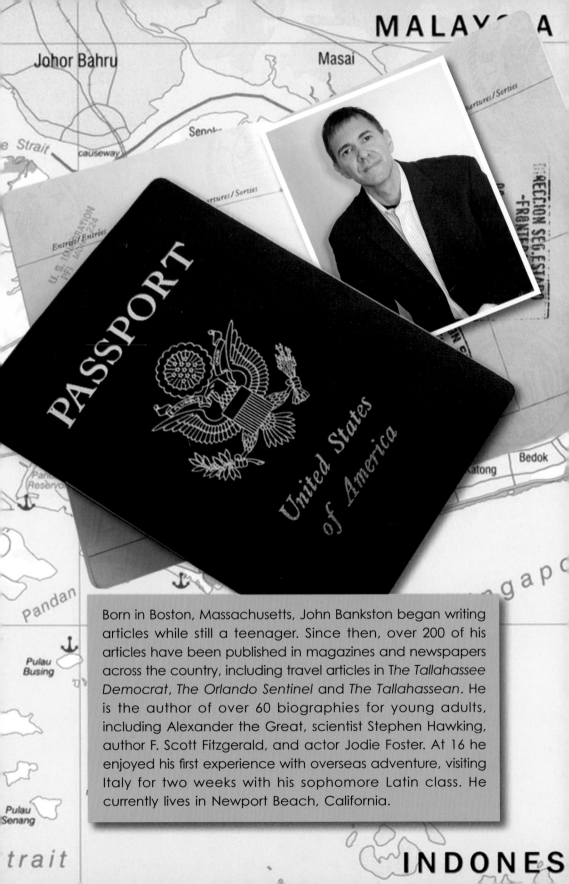

Born in Boston, Massachusetts, John Bankston began writing articles while still a teenager. Since then, over 200 of his articles have been published in magazines and newspapers across the country, including travel articles in *The Tallahassee Democrat*, *The Orlando Sentinel* and *The Tallahassean*. He is the author of over 60 biographies for young adults, including Alexander the Great, scientist Stephen Hawking, author F. Scott Fitzgerald, and actor Jodie Foster. At 16 he enjoyed his first experience with overseas adventure, visiting Italy for two weeks with his sophomore Latin class. He currently lives in Newport Beach, California.